Masters of Disguise: A

Elsie Belback

Rourke
Educational Media

rourkeeducationalmedia.com

Scan for Related Titles
and Teacher Resources

Before & After Reading Activities

Level: **J**   Word Count: **413 Words**
100th word: *survives* page 6

Teaching Focus:
Endings –ing- Locate the words jumping and tricking in the book. Write the words and underline the common root word. How does the ending change the meaning of the root word? Practice using the ending with another root word.

Before Reading:

Building Academic Vocabulary and Background Knowledge
Before reading a book, it is important to set the stage for your child or student by using pre-reading strategies. This will help them develop their vocabulary, increase their reading comprehension, and make connections across the curriculum.

1. Read the title and look at the cover. Let's make predictions about what this book will be about.
2. Take a picture walk by talking about the pictures/photographs in the book. Implant the vocabulary as you take the picture walk. Be sure to talk about the text features such as headings, Table of Contents, glossary, bolded words, captions, charts/diagrams, or Index.
3. Have students read the first page of text with you then have students read the remaining text.
4. Strategy Talk – use to assist students while reading.
   - Get your mouth ready
   - Look at the picture
   - Think…does it make sense
   - Think…does it look right
   - Think…does it sound right
   - Chunk it – by looking for a part you know
5. Read it again.
6. After reading the book complete the activities below.

Content Area Vocabulary
Use glossary words in a sentence.

harmless
insect
mimic
predators
prey
risk

After Reading:

Comprehension and Extension Activity
After reading the book, work on the following questions with your child or students in order to check their level of reading comprehension and content mastery.

1. Why do animals try to look like other things? (Asking questions)
2. What are predators? (Summarize)
3. How does a ghost mantis survive? (Summarize)
4. What does mimic mean? Do you mimic anything? (Text to self connection)

Extension Activity
Mimicry is when one animal mimics another in order to survive. Think of two animals or insects. How would one mimic the other? What would be the advantages of mimicking the other animal? Draw a picture of the two animals and what the mimicry would look like. Then provide a caption explaining why the mimicry would help with survival.

Step one. Step two. Step three.

Just like me.

You **mimic** your teacher's moves.

Animals can mimic, too!

Copy Cats

In nature, animals face many challenges. Animals have to find food. They have to hide from **predators**.

Brown Leaf Chameleon

Butterfly

Some animals mimic other things. They pretend to be more dangerous or less tasty. If an animal can trick a predator, it will survive another day.

Frogfish

Lots of sea creatures live in coral reefs. They flit and dart about. But wait, that's not coral! It's a frogfish waiting to gobble up small fish.

The frogfish looks like **harmless** coral. It survives by tricking **prey**.

WHERE THEY LIVE

North America, Europe, Asia, Africa, South America, Australia, Atlantic Ocean, Pacific Ocean, Indian Ocean

Frogfish

Frogfish

Walking Stick

Walking Stick

Does that twig have legs? It's not a twig at all. It's an **insect** called a walking stick. Walking sticks hide among the leaves and branches.

The walking stick does not look good to eat. It survives by tricking predators.

WHERE THEY LIVE

North America · Europe · Asia · Africa · South America · Australia
Atlantic Ocean · Pacific Ocean · Indian Ocean

■ Walking Stick

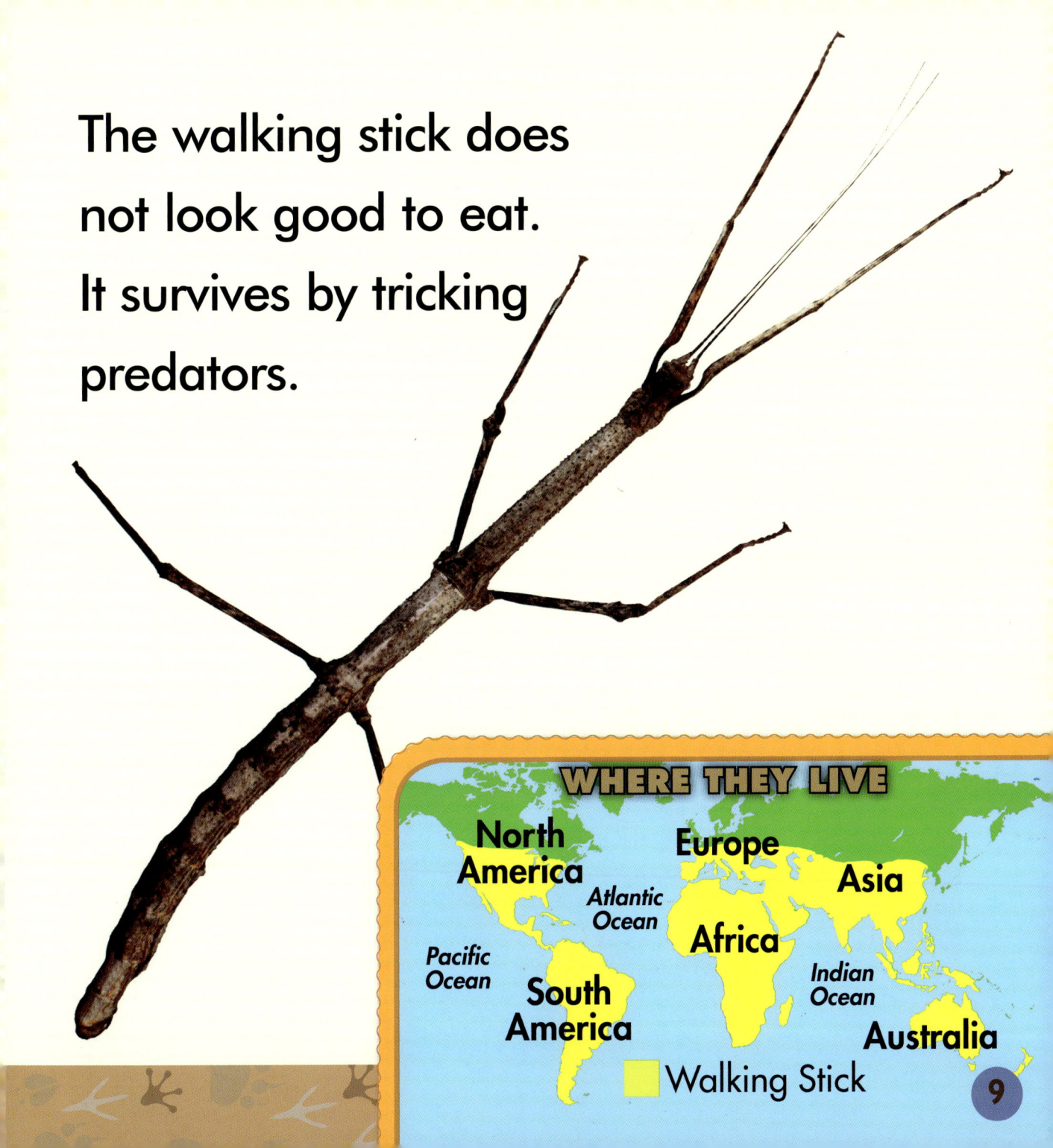

9

Mimic Octopus

Is it a sea snake? A jellyfish? A stingray? The mimic octopus pretends to be many animals. It changes shape to scare off predators or lure in a tasty meal.

Mimic Octopus

The mimic octopus can look like a friendly fish. It can also look very dangerous. It survives by tricking both predators and prey.

WHERE THEY LIVE

Pacific Ocean
Indian Ocean
Australia
Mimic Octopus

The mimic octopus mimics a fish swimming at the bottom of the ocean.

Metalmark Moth

Jumping spiders can hop into the air. They grab flying insects to eat. The metalmark moth folds its wings. It looks like a big spider.

The metalmark moth can look like a jumping spider. It survives by tricking predators.

WHERE THEY LIVE

Costa Rica
Pacific Ocean
Atlantic Ocean
South America
Metalmark Moth

Metalmark moths can be found worldwide, but scientists discovered the moths mimicking spiders in Costa Rica.

Metalmark Moth

Jumping Spider

13

Northern Pygmy Owl

Those aren't really eyes on the back of the owl's head. It just looks that way. Even when its back is turned, predators think the northern pygmy owl is watching.

The pygmy owl always looks like it is awake. It survives by tricking predators.

Northern Pygmy Owl

WHERE THEY LIVE

North America

Pacific Ocean

Northern Pygmy Owl

15

Ghost Mantis

In the fallen leaves a ghost mantis is hard to spot. The mantis waits there for its prey. It hides from insect-eating predators.

The ghost mantis looks like a dried up leaf. It survives by tricking both predators and prey.

Ghost Mantis

WHERE THEY LIVE

Africa
Atlantic Ocean
☐ Ghost Mantis

Most ghost mantises are shades of brown but they can also be green. Their color matches their environment.

17

Giant Swallowtail

The giant swallowtail caterpillar hides in plain sight. But few birds would **risk** taking a bite of the small grub. It looks just like bird poop!

Giant Swallowtail

WHERE THEY LIVE

North America

Pacific Ocean

Atlantic Ocean

Giant Swallowtail

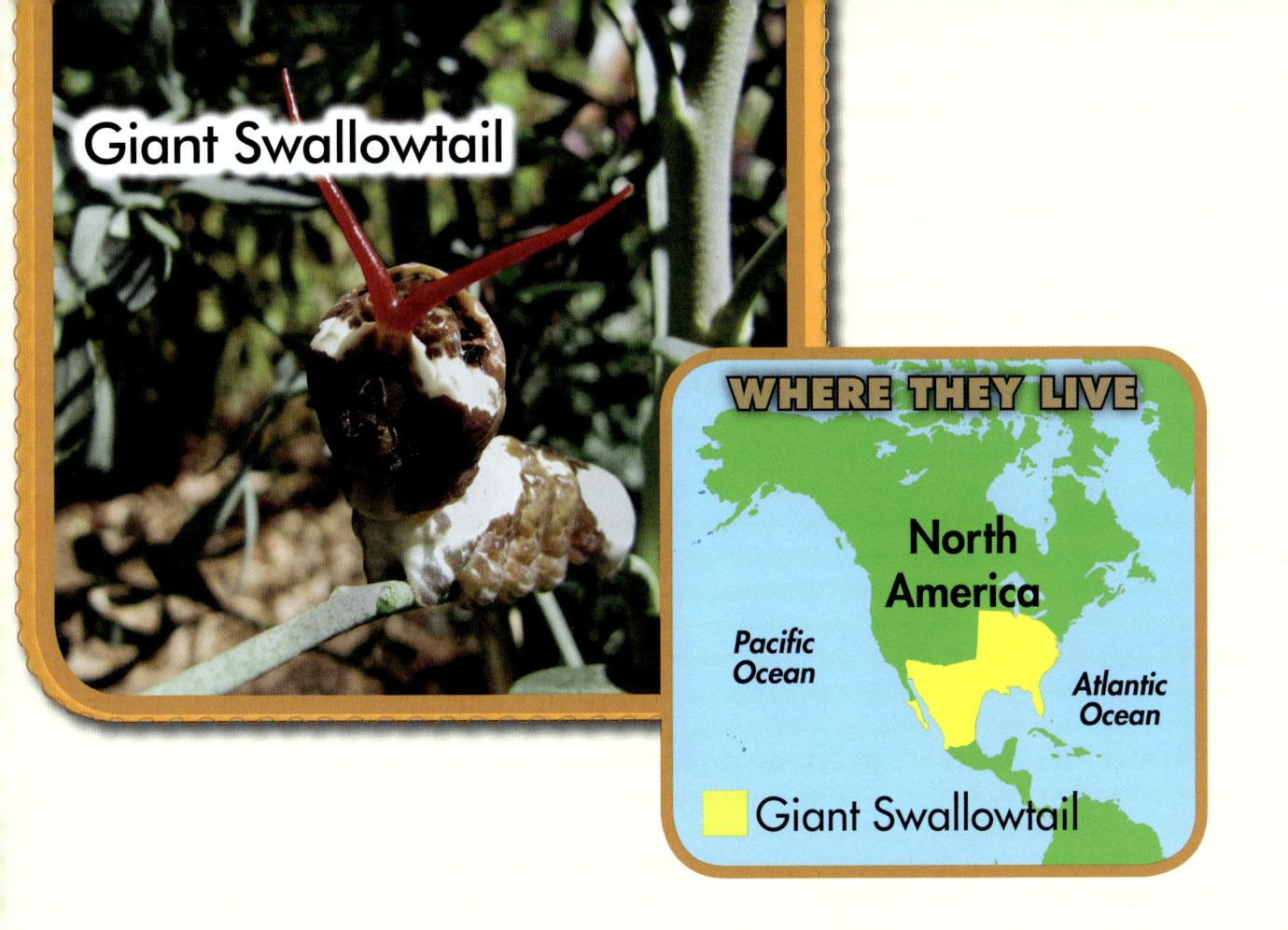

The giant swallowtail caterpillar does not look good to eat. It survives by tricking predators.

Torpedo Bug

In the forest, many plants are covered with leaves. The torpedo bug blends right in with the plants around it.

The torpedo bug looks like an ordinary leaf. It survives by tricking predators.

Torpedo bugs are originally from Australia, but have spread to such places as New Zealand, Hawaii, and California.

WHERE THEY LIVE

Asia

North America

Pacific Ocean

Atlantic Ocean

Indian Ocean

☐ Torpedo Bug

Australia

South America

If an animal looks like a good copy of something else, it can fool predators and prey in the wild.

Torpedo Bug

Photo Glossary

harmless (HAHRM-lis): Something that is harmless is not likely to cause injury or damage.

insect (IN-sekt): An insect is a small animal with three sets of legs. Insects are also called bugs.

mimic (MIM-ik): When you mimic something you imitate or copy it.

predators (PRED-uh-turz): Predators are animals that hunt other animals as food.

prey (pray): Prey is an animal that is hunted by other animals for food.

risk (risk): When you do something that is a risk, there is a chance that you will be injured or be harmed.

Index

caterpillar 18, 19
coral reefs 6
insect(s) 8, 12, 16
mimic 3, 5, 10, 11
predators 4, 9, 10, 11, 12, 14, 15, 16, 19, 20, 21
prey 6, 11, 16, 21

About the Author

Elsie Belback lives and writes in Brooklyn, New York. She is an educator, children's book writer, and life-long learner. Elsie has seen a walking stick at the Audubon Insectarium in New Orleans, Louisiana, but she knows she would never be able to spot one in the wild.

Meet The Author!
www.meetREMauthors.com

Websites

www.maniacworld.com/octopus-master-of-disguises.html
ngm.nationalgeographic.com/2009/08/mimicry/mimicry-interactive
www.bugfacts.net

© 2015 Rourke Educational Media

All rights reserved. No part of this book may be reproduced or utilized in any form or by any means, electronic or mechanical including photocopying, recording, or by any information storage and retrieval system without permission in writing from the publisher.

www.rourkeeducationalmedia.com

PHOTO CREDITS: Cover: ©semet; title page: ©katoosha; page 3, 23: ©Scott Griessel; page 4: ©reptiles4all; page 5: ©TAGSTOCK1; page 7, 23: ©Silke Baron; page 8, 23: ©i.fario; page 9: ©lucato; page 10, 24 (top): ©Andreas R. Mueller; page 11: ©orlandin; page 12: ©Muhamad Firdaus (inset), ©Susan Aceto; page 14: ©Alisonbowden; page 15: ©Hnoel; page 17: ©Cathy Keifer; page 18, 23 (bottom): ©Tyler Fox; page 19: ©Kelly Ballard; page 21: ©Chad Zuber; page 24: ©Hotshotsworldwide (middle)

Edited by: Jill Sherman
Cover design by: Jen Thomas
Interior design by: Rhea Magaro

Library of Congress PCN Data

Masters of Disguise: Animal Mimicry / Elsie Belback
(Close-Up on Amazing Animals)
ISBN (hard cover)(alk. paper) 978-1-62717-636-1
ISBN (soft cover) 978-1-62717-758-0
ISBN (e-Book) 978-1-62717-879-2
Library of Congress Control Number: 2014934204

Printed in the United States of America, North Mankato, Minnesota

Also Available as:
Rourke's e-Books